FAIR ISLE
BASICS & BEYOND™

Edited by Kara Gott Warner

HOUSE of
WHITE
BIRCHES

PUBLISHERS
SINCE 1947

Introduction

Fair Isle knitting is a traditional technique used to create patterns consisting of multiple colors. Named after Fair Isle, a tiny island in the north of Scotland, traditional Fair Isle patterns use a variety of colors and shades, using only two colors per row, and are generally knitted in the round without the use of the purl stitch.

In traditional Fair Isle knitting there are always two available active colors of yarn at a time; one is used to create the knit stitch and the other is carried loosely behind the work. Fair Isle patterns usually use only up to five stitches of one color at a time because too many stitches of the same color will leave a very long strand of carried yarn.

You'll often find that the term "Fair Isle" is used very generically, referring to any knitting where colors are alternated, leaving the unused yarns carried along the wrong side of the work. This is commonly termed "stranded colorwork," which is a more generic way to describe this technique, and has opened the door to a variety of colorwork options.

In *Fair Isle Basics & Beyond*, you'll discover 17 projects that incorporate a variation of Fair Isle and contemporary stranded-colorwork applications. We've assembled a collection of stylish accessory designs to help you get your bearings. In First Things First, try your hand on some simple two-color approaches using chunky- and worsted-weight yarns. Then, when you're ready to spread your wings, you can test your skills on the projects in Second Steps, which expands into using some lighter-gauge yarns and incorporating up to five colors with detailed color charts.

The variety of projects in *Fair Isle Basics & Beyond* will continually hone your colorworking skills, and keep your family and friends toasty warm in the winter months ahead!

Keep it colorful!

Kara

Kara Gott Warner, Editor

Table of Contents

Argyle Cowl & Cap,
page 17

Eileann Scarflette &
Fingerless Mitts,
page 21

Electric Butterfly,
page 39

Sweet Hearts,
page 33

FIRST THINGS FIRST

Striking yet simple to knit, these bold patterns with minimal color changes make stranded colorwork knitting accessible to everyone. Travel from Lerwick in the Northern Isles and out across the Moors of Scotland whilst these hats, mitts and cowls keep the cold wind at bay.

Fairburn Fingerless Mitts & Ski Band

Both fashionable and functional, this ski band and fingerless mitts are a casual and contemporary look. With simple colorwork accents, these are easy to make and wear.

Designs by Sara Louise Harper

Skill Level

 INTERMEDIATE

Sizes

Adult small/medium (medium/large) Instructions are given for smaller size, with larger size in parentheses. When only 1 number is given, it applies to both sizes.

Finished Measurements

Ski band circumference: 20 (22) inches
Mitts circumference: 7½ (8½) inches
Mitts length: 7¾ (8¾) inches

Materials

- Cascade 220 (worsted weight; 100% Peruvian highland wool; 220 yds/ 100g per skein): 1 skein each sienna #7821 (MC) and brown/gray multi #9539 (CC)
- Mitts: size 4 (3.5mm) double-point needles or size needed to obtain gauge
- Ski band: 2 size 4 (3.5mm) 24-inch circular needles or size needed to obtain gauge
- Size E/4 (3.5mm) crochet hook
- Stitch markers, 1 in CC for beg of rnd

4 MEDIUM

Gauge

20 sts and 24 rnds = 4 inches/10cm in 2-color stranded St st.

To save time, take time to check gauge.

Special Technique

Provisional Cast-On: With crochet hook and waste yarn, make a chain several sts longer than desired cast-on. With knitting needle and project yarn, pick up indicated number of sts in the "bumps" on back of chain. When indicated in pat, "unzip" the crochet chain and place live sts on needle.

Mitts

Left Mitt

With dpns and MC, cast on 40 (44) sts; mark beg of rnd and join, taking care not to twist sts.

Work 15 rnds in k1, p1 rib, inc 4 sts evenly on last rnd—44 (48) sts.

Set-up rnd: K22 (24) following Checkerboard Chart, place marker; k22 (24) following Diagonal Chart for left mitt.

Work 11 more rnds in established pats, ending at beg of rnd marker.

Thumb opening: Turn and work 10 rows back and forth for thumb opening, ending with a RS row.

Rejoin to work in the round; work even in established pats until mitt measures 7 (8) inches or ¾ inch shorter than desired length. Cut CC.

With MC, work 4 rnds in k1, p1 rib.

Bind off in rib.

Thumb

With MC and dpns, pick up and knit 20 sts around thumb opening.

Work 14 rnds (or to desired length) in k1, p1 rib.

Bind off in rib.

Right Mitt

Work as for left mitt to thumb opening, but work Diagonal Chart for right mitt.

Thumb opening: Work to first marker, then turn and work 10 full rows back and forth, ending with a RS row.

Complete as for left mitt.

Ski Band

Using Provisional Cast-On method, circular needle and MC, cast on 100 (108) sts; mark beg of rnd and join, taking care not to twist sts.

Work Checkerboard pat following chart until piece measures 3 inches or desired width. Note the number of rnds worked in Checkerboard pat.

With MC only, knit 2 rnds.

Work Diagonal pat following either chart until you have worked same number of rnds as for the Checkerboard pat.

With MC only, knit 1 rnd.

Finishing

Unzip Provisional Cast-On and put sts on 2nd circular needle. With RS facing out, graft sts tog using Kitchener st.

Weave in all ends. Block. ●

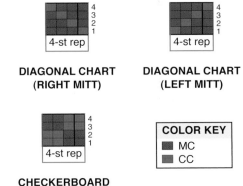

DIAGONAL CHART (RIGHT MITT)

DIAGONAL CHART (LEFT MITT)

CHECKERBOARD CHART

COLOR KEY
■ MC
■ CC

Lerwick Leg Warmers & Skullcap

This duo does the job fashionably well with two-tone diamond colorwork patterning.

Designs by Amy Polcyn

. . . .

Skill Level

 INTERMEDIATE

Size
Woman's medium

Finished Measurements
Leg warmers circumference: 14 inches
Leg warmers length: 15 inches
Skullcap circumference: 19 inches
(stretches to fit)

Materials
- Stitch Nation by Debbie Stoller Full o' Sheep (Aran weight; 100% wool; 155 yds/100g per ball): 2 balls passionfruit #2925 (MC), 1 ball ocean #2820 (CC)
- Size 8 (5mm) 16-inch circular and double-point needles (set of 5) or size needed to obtain gauge
- Stitch marker

Gauge
16 sts and 21 rnds = 4 inches/10cm in St st.

17 sts and 21 rnds = 4 inches/10cm in 2-color stranded St st.

To save time, take time to check gauge.

Leg Warmers

With dpns and MC, cast on 52 sts; mark beg of rnd and join, being careful not to twist sts.

Work in k2, p2 rib for 2 inches; inc 8 sts evenly on last rnd—60 sts.

Change to St st and knit 1 rnd.

Work 56 rnds (2 reps) in Fair Isle pat following chart.

Change to MC and work in k2, p2 rib, dec 8 sts evenly around—52 sts.

Continue in rib for 2 inches.

Bind off in pat.

Weave in all ends.

Block.

Skullcap

With circular needle and MC, cast on 80 sts; place marker for beg of rnd and join, being careful not to twist sts.

Work in k2, p2 rib for 1½ inches.

Change to St st and knit 1 rnd.

Work 28 rnds in Fair Isle pat following chart; on last rnd, place markers every 8 sts.

Shape crown
Note: Change to dpns when necessary.

Change to MC.

Dec rnd: [Knit to marker, k2tog] 10 times—70 sts.

Rep Dec rnd [every other rnd] 5 more times—20 sts.

Last rnd: [K2tog] 10 times—10 sts.

Cut yarn, leaving a 6-inch tail; thread yarn through rem sts and pull tight to secure.

Finishing
Weave in all ends. Block. ●

COLOR KEY
- ■ MC
- ■ CC

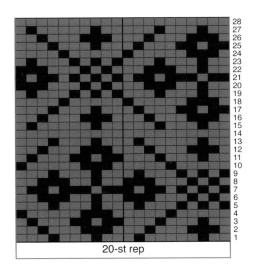

20-st rep

FAIR ISLE CHART

Northern Isles

Learn the ropes of stranded colorwork when you make these simple mittens with a floral border.

Design by Sara Harper

· ·

Skill Level

 INTERMEDIATE

Sizes
Adult's small/medium (medium/large)
Instructions are given for smaller size, with larger size in parentheses. When only 1 number is given, it applies to both sizes.

Finished Measurements
Circumference: 7½ (8½) inches
Length: 8 (9) inches

Materials
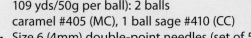
- Zitron Nimbus (worsted weight; 100% organic merino wool; 109 yds/50g per ball): 2 balls caramel #405 (MC), 1 ball sage #410 (CC)
- Size 6 (4mm) double-point needles (set of 5) or size needed to obtain gauge
- Stitch holder
- Stitch marker

Gauge
24 sts and 28 rnds = 4 inches/10cm in 2-color stranded St st.

To save time, take time to check gauge.

Special Abbreviations
N1, N2, N3, N4: Needle 1, Needle 2, Needle 3 and Needle 4.

Left Mitten

Cuff
With CC, cast on 40 (48) sts and distribute evenly on 4 dpns; mark beg of rnd and join, taking care not to twist sts.

Change to MC; knit 1 rnd.

Work 6 rnds in k2, p2 rib.

Change to St st and work 13-rnd Leaf pat following chart.

With MC, knit 10 rnds or desired length to beg of thumb opening.

Thumb opening rnd: K3; place next 5 sts on a holder for thumb; cast on 5 sts using backward-loop method; knit to end of rnd.

Knit all rnds until mitten measures 6 (6½) inches or 2 (2½) inches short of desired length, ending last rnd 10 (12) sts before beg of rnd marker. This will be new beg of rnd.

Mitten top
Dec rnd: N1: Ssk, knit to end; N2: knit to last 2 sts, k2tog; N3 and N4: work as for N1 and N2—36 (44) sts.

Rep Dec rnd [every 3rd rnd] twice more, then [every other rnd] 2 (3) times—20 (24) sts.

Slip sts from N1 to N2 and from N3 to N4. Graft top closed using Kitchener st.

Thumb
With CC and dpns, k5 from holder, then pick up and knit 9 (11) sts around opening—14 (16) sts.

Mark beg of rnd and join; work in St st until thumb measures 1¾ inches or ½ inch short of desired thumb length, ending last rnd 1 (2) st(s) before beg of rnd marker.

Redistribute sts on 4 needles as follows: 3-4-3-4 (4-4-4-4).

Dec rnd: N1: Ssk, knit to end; N2: knit to last 2 sts, k2tog; N3 and N4: work as for N1 and N2—10 (12) sts.

Rep Dec rnd [every other rnd] 1 (2) more time(s)—
6 (4) sts rem.

Cut yarn, leaving a 4-inch tail. Using tapestry needle,
thread tail through rem sts and pull tight.

Weave in all ends.

Block as desired.

Right Mitten
Work as for left mitten to thumb opening.

Thumb opening rnd: Knit to last 8 sts; place
next 5 sts on a holder for thumb; cast on 5 sts using
backward-loop method; knit to end of rnd.

Continue as for left mitten. ●

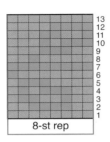

13
12
11
10
9
8
7
6
5
4
3
2
1

8-st rep

LEAF CHART

COLOR KEY
☐ MC
☐ CC

Scottish Moors Tube Scarf

From simplicity comes glamour in mossy and bright green shades; this piece is a showstopper.

Design by Lisa Ellis

· ·

Skill Level
■ ■ ■ ▢ INTERMEDIATE

Finished Size
6 x 59 inches (excluding fringe)

Materials
- Cascade 220 Superwash (worsted weight; 100% superwash wool; 220 yds/100g per skein): 2 skeins dark green #865 (A); 1 skein each lime green #886 (B), medium green #891 (C) and leaf green #888 (D)
- Size 7 (4.5mm) 16-inch circular needle or size needed to obtain gauge
- Size H/8 (5mm) crochet hook
- 4 stitch markers, 1 in CC for beg of rnd

Gauge
20 sts and 22 rnds = 4 inches/10cm in 2-color stranded St st.

Exact gauge is not critical for this project.

Pattern Notes
Scarf is knit in the round with open ends like a tube.

If knitting becomes too tight on the 16-inch circular needle, go up one size needle or change to double-point needles, Magic Loop or 2 circular needles as needed to work in the round.

To keep the stranded knitting from puckering, keep the carried yarns loose by knitting the scarf inside out or by spreading the stitches across the knitting needle.

Scarf
With A, cast on 70 sts; place marker for beg of rnd and join, taking care not to twist sts.

Set-up rnd: *P1, k17, place marker to mark pat rep, k17, place marker for side edge; rep from * once, ending at beg of rnd marker.

Join B; *p1 in A; following chart, work Honeycomb pat over the next 34 sts, slip marker; rep from * once more.

Continue working chart with A and B until 6-rnd pat has been worked 17 times. Cut B.

Join C; continue in established pat, working with A and C until 6-rnd pat has been worked 17 times. Cut C.

Join D; continue in established pat, working with A and D until 6-rnd pat has been worked 17 times. Cut D.

With A, knit 1 rnd.

Bind off all sts very loosely.

Cut A, leaving a 3-inch tail.

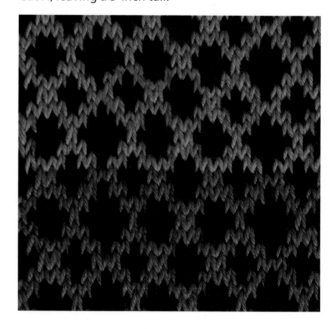

Finishing

Weave in all ends. Block to finished measurements, using the purl sts as the fold line.

Fringe

Cut 60 (14-inch) strands of A.

*Fold 5 strands in half. With RS facing and beg below first diamond motif, use crochet hook to draw folded end through both pieces of fabric from front to back. Pull loose ends through folded section. Draw up knot firmly. Rep from *, placing 6 evenly spaced fringes along each short edge below the diamond motifs. Trim even. ●

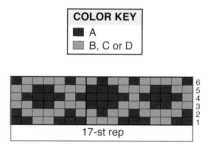

COLOR KEY
■ A
▨ B, C or D

HONEYCOMB CHART

17-st rep

Argyle Cowl & Cap

Make a bold statement in this bulky-weight graphic cap and cowl.

Designs by Kate Atherley

. . . .

Skill Level
■■■□ INTERMEDIATE

Cowl
Size
One size fits all

Finished Measurements
Circumference: 24 inches
Length: 8½ inches

Materials
• Schoppel Wolle XL (bulky weight; 100% merino wool; 72 yds/100g per hank): 1 hank each black #0880 (A) and white chocolate #0980 (B)
• Size 11 (8mm) 16-inch circular needle or size needed to obtain gauge
• Stitch marker

Cap
Sizes
Adult's small (medium, large) Instructions are given for smallest size, with larger sizes in parentheses. When only 1 number is given, it applies to all sizes.

Finished Measurements
Circumference: 20 (22, 24) inches
Length: 8 (8½, 9¼) inches

Materials
• Schoppel Wolle XL (bulky weight; 100% merino wool, 72 yds/100g per hank): 1 hank each black #0880 (A) and white chocolate #0980 (B)
• Cap sizes small and large: size 11 (8mm) 16-inch circular and double-point needles (set of 5) or size needed to obtain gauge
• Cap size medium: size 13 (9mm) 16-inch circular and double-point needles (set of 5) or size needed to obtain gauge
• Stitch marker

Cowl

Gauge
12 sts and 16 rnds = 4 inches/10cm in 2-color stranded St st.

To save time, take time to check gauge.

Pattern Note
The pattern stitch begins with 1 stitch of A on all rounds to avoid a color jog.

Cowl
With circular needle and A, cast on 50 sts; place marker to mark beg of rnd and join, taking care not to twist sts.

Work 2 rnds in k1, p1 rib.

Knit 1 rnd, inc 23 sts evenly around—73 sts.

Join B and work 21 rnds of Argyle pat following chart, ending with Rnd 1. Cut B.

With A, knit 1 rnd.

Next rnd: K1, p1, [k2tog, p1] 12 times, k1, p1, [k2tog, p1] 11 times—50 sts.

Work 1 rnd in k1, p1 rib.

Bind off in rib.

Finishing
Weave in all ends. Block.

Cap

Gauge
12 sts and 16 rnds = 4 inches/10cm in 2-color stranded St st using smaller needles.

11 sts and 15 rnds = 4 inches/10cm in 2-color stranded St st using larger needles.

To save time, take time to check gauge.

Pattern Notes

The pattern stitch begins with 1 stitch of A on all rounds to avoid a color jog.

When working crown, change to double-point needles when stitches no longer fit comfortably on circular needle.

Cap

Using circular needle for appropriate size and A, cast on 44 (44, 50) sts; mark beg of rnd and join, taking care not to twist sts.

Work 2 rnds in k1, p1 rib.

Knit 1 rnd, inc 17 (17, 23) sts evenly around—61 (61, 73) sts.

Knit 0 (1, 2) rnd(s).

Join B and work 11 rnds of Argyle pat following chart, ending with Rnd 1. Cut B.

Knit 2 (3, 3) rnds with A, dec 1 st on last rnd—60 (60, 72) sts.

Crown

Rnd 1: *K8 (8, 10), k2tog, place marker; rep from * around—54 (54, 66) sts.

Rnd 2: Knit around.

Rnd 3 (dec rnd): *Knit to 2 sts before marker, k2tog; rep from * around—48 (48, 60) sts.

Rep [Rnds 2 and 3] 7 (7, 9) times—6 sts.

Cut yarn, leaving a 6-inch tail. Using tapestry needle, thread tail through rem sts and pull tight.

Finishing

Weave in all ends. Block. ●

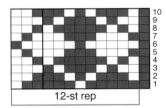

COLOR KEY
■ A
□ B

12-st rep

ARGYLE CHART

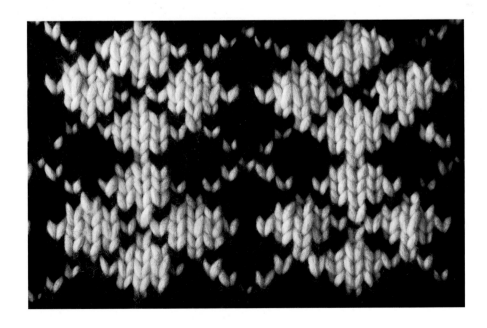

SECOND STEPS

This chapter presents a captivating collection of projects that employ multiple color combinations from the whimsy of Happy Little Fish Hat & Mittens and Electric Butterfly to the elegant Eileann Scarflette & Fingerless Mitts. These delightful and vibrant designs will quickly become well-loved family heirlooms.

Eileann Scarflette & Fingerless Mitts

This artfully patterned creation will be one you'll wish you could wear all year long.

Designs by Irina Poludnenko

Skill Level
 INTERMEDIATE

Sizes
Mitts
Adult's small/medium (medium/large)
Instructions are given for smaller size, with larger size in parentheses. When only 1 number is given, it applies to both sizes.

Scarflette
1 size

Finished Measurements
Mitt circumference: 7 (7¾) inches
Scarflette: 4 x 32 inches

Materials
- Rowan Felted Tweed DK (DK weight; 50% merino wool/25% alpaca/ 25% viscose; 191 yds/ 50g per ball): 1 ball each avocado #161 (A), rage #150 (B), seasalter #178 (C), gilt #160 (D), bilberry #151 (E) and ginger #154 (F)
- Size 3 (3.25mm) double-point needles or size needed to obtain gauge
- Size D/3 (3.25mm) crochet hook
- Stitch markers, 1 in CC for beg of rnd
- Stitch holder

Gauge
25 sts and 28 rnds = 4 inches/10cm 2-colors stranded St st.

To save time, take time to check gauge.

Special Abbreviations
Make 1 Left (M1L): Insert LH needle from front to back under the running thread between the last st worked and next st on LH needle; knit into the back of resulting loop.

Make 1 Right (M1R): Insert LH needle from back to front under the running thread between the last st worked and next st on LH needle. With RH needle, knit into the front of resulting loop.

Make 1 Purlwise (M1P): Insert LH needle from front to back under the running thread between the last st worked and next st on RH needle; purl into the back of resulting loop.

Special Techniques
Picot Bind-Off: *Bind off 2 sts, slip rem st from RH to LH needle; using cable method, cast on 2 sts; bind off 1, k2tog, bind off 1; rep from *.

Provisional Cast-On: With crochet hook and waste yarn, make a chain several sts longer than desired cast-on. With knitting needle and project yarn, pick up indicated number of sts in the "bumps" on back of chain. When indicated in pattern, "unzip" the crochet chain to free live sts.

Fingerless Mitts

Cuff
With A, cast on 44 (48) sts; mark beg of rnd and join, taking care not to twist sts.

Work in k1, p1 rib for 2¾ inches.

Change to St st and work Rnds 1–10 of Mitt Chart.

Thumb gusset
Rnd 1: Working Rnd 11 of chart, k1, place marker for gusset, work to end of rnd.

Rnd 2: Continuing charted pat, M1R, k1, M1L, slip marker, work to end of rnd—3 thumb gusset sts.

Rnd 3: Work even in established pat.

Rnd 4 (inc rnd): Continuing in charted pat, M1R, knit to marker, M1L, slip marker, work to end of rnd—5 thumb gusset sts.

Rep [Rnds 3 and 4] 8 (9) more times—21 (23) thumb gusset sts.

Work even (if necessary) until Rnd 33 of pat is complete.

Next rnd: Sl 21 (23) gusset sts between markers to holder; cast on 1 st, work in pat to end of rnd—44 (48) sts.

Upper hand
Work even in pat to end of chart.

With A, work Picot Bind-Off.

Thumb
Transfer gusset sts to dpns; with D, pick up and knit 3 (1) st(s) in cast-on st, then work in pat around—24 sts.

Continue in charted pat through Rnd 41.

With A, work Picot Bind-Off.

Scarflette

Using Provisional Cast-On method and D, cast on 84 sts; mark beg of rnd and join, taking care not to twist sts.

Work 15 rnds in k1, p2 rib.

Dec rnd: *K1, p2tog; rep from * around—56 sts.

Work 7 rnds in k1, p1 rib.

Change to St st and work [Rnds 1–77 of Scarflette Chart] twice.

Work Rnds 1–21 following Scarflette Chart.

Next rnd (make opening): [Work 16 sts in pat, bind off 12 sts] twice.

Next rnd: [Work 16 sts in pat, cast on 12 sts] twice.

Continue in pat through Rnd 34 of chart.

Change to E; work 7 rnds in k1, p1 rib.

Inc rnd: *K1, p1, M1P; rep from * around—84 sts.

Work 15 rnds in k1, p2 rib.

With A, work Picot Bind-Off.

Unzip Provisional Cast-On and transfer live sts to dpns.

With E, work Picot Bind-Off.

Finishing

With B, pick up and knit 24 sts around 1 side's opening. Bind off kwise.

Rep around opening on other side.

Sew both openings tog to create a hole.

Weave in all ends. Block. ●

COLOR KEY

▨	K with A
▨	K with B
■	K with C
☐	K with D
▨	K with E
▨	K with F
–	P with color indicated

MITT CHART

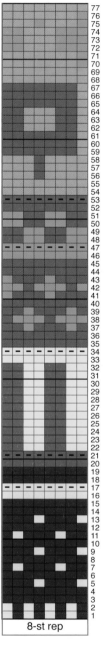

SCARFLETTE CHART

Leafy Flap Hat & Flip-Top Mittens

Both fashionable and functional, this set will add color to the wintry landscape.

Designs by Lynne LeBlanc

· ·

Skill Level
■■■◗ EXPERIENCED

Sizes
Child's medium/large (adult's small/medium) Instructions are given for smaller size, with larger size in parentheses. When only 1 number is given, it applies to both sizes.

Finished Measurements
Hat circumference: 19 (21) inches
Hat height: 8 (8½) inches
Mittens circumference: 6 (9) inches
Mittens length: 8 (9) inches

Materials
- Berroco Comfort DK (DK weight; 50% super fine nylon/50% super fine acrylic; 178 yds/50g per ball): 2 balls lovage #2761 (A); 1 ball each sprig #2721 (B), teaberry #2730 (C), filbert #2745 (D) and purple #2722 (E)
- Size 4 (3.5mm) 16-inch circular needle
- Size 5 (3.75mm) 16-inch circular and double-point (set of 5) needles or size needed to obtain gauge
- Spare needle, size 4 or smaller
- Size F/5 (3.75mm) crochet hook
- Stitch marker
- Stitch holders
- 2 (⅝-inch) buttons (for mittens)

Gauge
24 sts and 32 rnds = 4 inches/10cm in stranded 2-color St st with larger needles.

To save time, take time to check gauge.

Special Abbreviations
Knit in front and back (kfb): Knit in front and back of a st to inc 1.

Knit in back and front (kbf): Knit in back and front of a st to inc 1.

Make 1 Left (M1L): Insert LH needle from front to back under the running thread between the last st worked and next st on LH needle; knit into the back of resulting loop.

Make 1 Right (M1R): Insert LH needle from back to front under the running thread between the last st worked and next st on LH needle. With RH needle, knit into the front of resulting loop.

Special Technique
Provisional Cast-On: With crochet hook and waste yarn, make a chain several sts longer than desired cast-on. With knitting needle and project yarn, pick up indicated number of sts in the "bumps" on back of chain. When indicated in pat, "unzip" the crochet chain and place live sts on needle.

Pattern Notes
When working hat, change to double-point needles when stitches no longer fit comfortably on circular needle.

Lower part of mitten follows Hat Chart.

The mitten cuff is worked flat; the rest of the cuff is worked in the round.

The zigzag motif is a 6-stitch repeat; the leaf motif is a 14-stitch repeat.

Hat

Earflaps
Make 2

With A and larger needle, cast on 3 (5) sts.

Following Earflap Chart, knit 1 row, purl 1 row, then inc 2 sts at each side [every RS row] 4 times as follows: K1, kfb, M1L, knit to last 2 sts, M1R, kbf, k1—19 (21) sts.

Work even until Earflap Chart is complete.

Cut yarn and put sts on holder.

Body
With larger circular needle, E and using Provisional Cast-On method, cast on 14 (17) sts; knit across 19 (21) earflap sts; provisionally cast on 48 (50) sts; knit across 19 (21) earflap sts; cast on 14 (17) sts; mark beg of rnd (center back) and join, taking care not to twist sts—114 (126) sts.

Knit 1 rnd.

Work first 8 rnds of Hat Chart.

Next rnd: Work Rnd 9 and dec 2 (0) sts evenly around—112 (126) sts.

Continue Hat Chart, ending with Rnd 24.

Next rnd: Work Rnd 25, inc 2 (0) sts evenly around—114 (126) sts.

Continue Hat Chart, ending with Rnd 32.

Next rnd: Work Rnd 33, dec 2 (0) sts evenly around—112 (126) sts.

Complete Hat Chart, working double-dec as indicated—16 (18) sts.

Cut B, leaving a 6-inch tail. Using tapestry needle, thread tail through rem sts, and pull tight. Secure tail on WS.

Ribbed edging
Unzip Provisional Cast-On and put live sts on larger circular needle.

With RS facing, using smaller needle and A, beg at center back, k14 (17) to first earflap, pick up and knit 48 sts around earflap, k48 (50) across front, pick up and knit 48 sts around second earflap, and k14 (17) to center back—172 (180) sts.

Rnd 1: Work in k1, p1 rib around, dec 2 (0) sts evenly around—170 (180) sts.

Rnd 2: *Work in established rib to point where flap joins body, ending with a purl st; sk2p, then continue in rib around flap to next joining point, ending with a purl st, sk2p; rep from * once more—162 (172) sts.

Bind off all sts in rib.

Ties
Cut 12 strands of A, each approx 36 inches long.

Thread 6 strands through the bottom center st of 1 earflap and center them so you have 12 ends, 18 inches long each.

Divide into 3 groups of 4 and braid until tie is desired length; knot ends and trim to even length.

Rep on other flap.

Mittens

Left Mitten

Cuff
With smaller circular needle and A and using Provisional Cast-On method, cast on 35 (45) sts; do not join.

Row 1 (RS): Knit across.

Row 2 (WS): P1, *k1, p1; rep from * to end.

Work even in established rib until piece measures 3 (4) inches, ending with a WS row.

Joining row (RS): Unzip Provisional Cast-On and place live sts on spare needle. Fold piece in half so that cast-on edge is behind working needle. *Knit tog 1 st from working needle with 1 st from cast-on needle; rep from * across to join into a doubled fabric. Mark beg of rnd and join. *Note: Beg of rnd is at center of palm.*

Hand

Rnd 1: Change to larger dpns and E; work Rnd 1 of Hat Chart, inc 7 (9) sts evenly around—42 (54) sts.

Work Rnds 2–8 of Hat Chart.

Next rnd: Work Rnd 9, inc 0 (2) sts evenly around—42 (56) sts.

Continue Hat Chart, ending with Rnd 23.

Next rnd: Work Rnd 24, dec 0 (2) sts evenly around—42 (54) sts.

Thumb opening rnd: Working Rnd 25, k16 (19); transfer last 7 (9) sts worked to a holder for the thumb; knit to end of rnd.

Next rnd: Working Rnd 26, knit to sts on holder, cast on 7 (9) sts, knit to end of rnd.

Continue Hat Chart, ending with Rnd 31.

Flap opening rnd: With E, k11 (14) and transfer to holder; knit to end of rnd, then transfer last 10 (14) sts to same holder for lower flap opening—21 (26) back hand sts rem.

Next rnd: Change to A and Mitten Chart; provisionally cast on 11 (14) sts; knit across sts on needle and inc 0 (2) sts, provisionally cast on 10 (14) sts—42 (56) sts.

Work Mitten Chart, ending with Rnd 17.

Next rnd: Work Rnd 18, dec 2 (0) sts evenly around—40 (56) sts.

Complete Mitten Chart—10 (14) sts.

Cut yarn, leaving a 6-inch tail.

Using tapestry needle, thread tail through rem sts and pull tight.

Thumb

Transfer 7 (9) sts from holder to dpn.

With A and dpns, pick up and knit 7 (9) sts from cast-on sts, k7 (9)—14 (18) sts.

Mark beg of rnd.

Knit around until thumb measures 1½ (1¾) inches or desired length.

Dec rnd: [K2 (4), k2tog] 3 times, k2 (0)—11 (15) sts.

Knit 1 rnd.

For child's size
Next rnd: [K1, k2tog] 3 times, k2, [k2tog] 3 times, k2—5 sts.

For adult's size
Next rnd: [K4, k2tog] 3 times, [k3, k2tog] 3 times, [k1, k2tog] 3 times—6 sts.

For both sizes
Cut yarn, leaving a 6-inch tail.

Using tapestry needle, thread tail through rem sts and pull tight.

Lower flap opening
Transfer 21 (28) sts to smaller needle.

Row 1 (RS): Join A; knit across.

Row 2: P1 (0), *k1, p1; rep from * across.

Rows 3–5: Work in established rib.

Bind off loosely in rib.

Upper flap opening
Unzip Provisional Cast-On and put 21 (28) live sts on larger needle.

Row 1 (RS): Join E; k1, M1L, knit to last st, M1L, k1—23 (30) sts (first and last sts are selvedge sts).

Rows 2–7: Working back and forth in St st, work Rows 2–7 of Zigzag pat from Hat Chart.

Row 8: Change to A; purl across, dec 0 (1) st—23 (29) sts.

Row 9: K1, *p1, k1; rep from * across.

Bind off loosely in rib.

Right Mitten

Work as for left mitten to thumb opening.

Thumb opening rnd: Working Rnd 25, k26 (37); transfer last 7 (9) sts worked to a holder for the thumb; knit to end of rnd.

Continue as for left mitten to flap opening.

Flap opening rnd: With E, k10 (14) and transfer to holder; knit to end of rnd, then transfer last 11 (14) sts to same holder for lower flap opening—21 (26) back hand sts rem.

Complete hand as for left mitten.

Work thumb, lower and upper flap openings as for left mitten.

Finishing

Weave in all ends.

Sew mitten cuff seams.

With E and using mattress st, sew edges of upper flap opening to sides of mitten.

With crochet hook and B, and leaving 2-inch tails at either end, work a chain approx 1 inch long.

Form loop with chain, securing both tails to WS of center top of mitten.

Sew button to center of the back-hand side of mitten a little above the cuff. ●

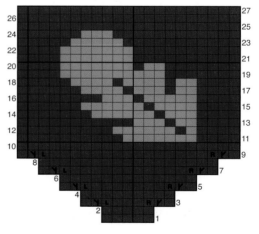

14-st rep, dec to 8-st rep

MITTEN CHART

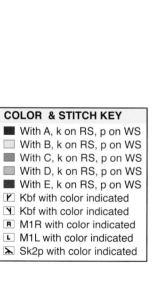

COLOR & STITCH KEY

- ■ With A, k on RS, p on WS
- □ With B, k on RS, p on WS
- ▨ With C, k on RS, p on WS
- ▨ With D, k on RS, p on WS
- ■ With E, k on RS, p on WS
- Ⓥ Kbf with color indicated
- Ⓨ Kbf with color indicated
- Ⓡ M1R with color indicated
- Ⓛ M1L with color indicated
- ⊠ Sk2p with color indicated

6-st rep

14-st rep

HAT CHART

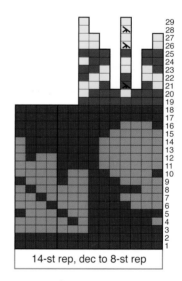

**EARFLAP CHART
(ADULT)**

Note: For child's size, cast on 3 sts and work incs at edges as for Adult chart; child's earflap will end with 2 fewer sts.

Happy Little Fish Hat & Mittens

Test your colorworking skills on this multicolored, whimsical under-the-sea set.

Designs by Simona Merchant-Dest

. . . .

Skill Level

■■■□ INTERMEDIATE

Sizes

Hat

Child's extra-small (small, medium, large) Instructions are given for smallest size, with larger sizes in parentheses. When only 1 number is given, it applies to all sizes.

Mittens

Child's small (medium, large) Instructions are given for smallest size, with larger sizes in parentheses. When only 1 number is given, it applies to all sizes.

Finished Measurements

Hat circumference: 14¾ (16¼, 17¾, 19¼) inches
Hat height: 5½ (6½, 7½, 8) inches
Mittens hand circumference: 4½ (6, 7½) inches
Mittens length: 6 (6¾, 7½) inches

Materials
- HiKoo Simplicity (DK weight; 55% superwash merino wool/28% acrylic/17% nylon; 117 yds/50g per hank): 2 hanks indigo #011 (A); 1 hank each natural olive #008 (B), iris blue #012 (C), chocolate milk #020 (D) and Sahara sand #019 (E)
- Size 4 (3.5mm) double-point needles (set of 4 or 5) or size needed to obtain gauge
- Size 5 (3.75mm) 16-inch circular (optional) and double-point (set of 5) needles or size needed to obtain gauge
- Stitch markers, 1 in CC for beg of rnd

3 LIGHT

Gauge

27 sts and 30 rnds = 4 inches/10cm in stranded St st.

To save time, take time to check gauge.

Special Abbreviation

Place marker (pm): Place a marker on needle to separate sections.

Pattern Notes

Hat is worked in the round from the rib edge to the crown.

Switch to double-point needles when stitches no longer fit comfortably on circular needle.

Hat

With B and smaller needle, cast on 100 (108, 120, 128) sts, pm for beg of rnd and join, taking care not to twist sts.

Work 8 rnds in k2, p2 rib.

Inc rnd: Knit, inc 0 (2, 0, 2) sts evenly around—100 (110, 120, 130) sts.

Switch to larger needle and work Fish pat following chart, ending ending with Rnd 23 (23, 32, 32).

Change to A and knit 0 (0, 2, 6) rnds.

Crown

Rnd 1: *K10, pm; rep from * around.

Rnd 2 (dec rnd): *Knit to 2 sts before marker, k2tog; rep from * around—90 (99, 108, 117) sts.

Rnd 3: Knit.

Rep [Rnds 2 and 3] 2 (1, 5, 5) more time(s)—70 (88, 48, 52) sts.

Rep [Rnd 2] 5 (6, 2, 2) times—20 (22, 24, 26) sts.

Next rnd: K2tog around—10 (11, 12, 13) sts.

Finishing

Cut yarn, leaving 5-inch tail. Using tapestry needle, thread tail through rem sts and pull tight. Weave in all ends. Block as necessary.

Mittens

Left Mitten

With smaller dpn and B, cast on 28 (40, 48) sts; pm for beg of rnd and join, taking care not to twist sts.

Work 6 (8, 8) rnds in k2, p2 rib and on last rnd, inc 2 (0, 2) sts evenly around—30 (40, 50) sts.

Rearrange sts as follows: N1: 7 (10, 12) sts; N2: 15 (20, 25) sts; N3: 8 (10, 13) sts.

Work Rnds 1–9 of Fish Chart.

With A, knit 2 rnds.

Thumb gusset

Rnd 1: K7 (10, 12), pm, M1, knit to end—31 (41, 51) sts.

Rnd 2: Knit to marker, slip marker, k1, M1, pm, knit to end—32 (42, 52) sts with 2 gusset sts between markers.

Rnd 3: Knit around.

Rnd 4 (inc rnd): Knit to first marker, slip marker, M1, knit to next marker, M1, knit to end—34 (44, 54) sts.

Rep [Rnds 3 and 4] 3 (4, 5) more times—40 (52, 64) sts with 10 (12, 14) gusset sts.

Next rnd: Removing markers when you come to them, knit to marker, place gusset sts on waste yarn without working them, knit to end—30 (40, 50) sts.

Work even in St st until piece measures approx 4½ (5½, 5¼) inches from cast-on edge.

Shape top

Rnd 1 (dec rnd): N1: Knit to last 2 sts, k2tog; N2: ssk, knit to last 2 sts, k2tog; N3: ssk, knit to end—26 (36, 46) sts.

Rnd 2: Knit around.

Rep [Rnds 1 and 2] twice more—18 (28, 38) sts.

Rep [Rnd 1] 2 (4, 6) times—10 (12, 14) sts.

Divide sts from N2 and transfer to N1 and N3 so that there are 5 (6, 7) sts on each needle.

Cut yarn, leaving a 10-inch tail. Using tapestry needle and tail, graft opening closed using Kitchener st.

Thumb

Divide 10 (12, 14) thumb gusset sts among 3 dpns; join A and pick up and knit 1 st in palm at base of thumb, pm for beg of rnd, pick up and knit 1 st at base of thumb, knit to end of rnd—12 (14, 16) sts.

Knit 10 (12, 13) rnds.

Next rnd: [K6 (7, 8), pm] twice.

Dec rnd: [Ssk, knit to 2 sts before marker, k2tog] twice—8 (10, 12) sts.

Rep Dec rnd 0 (0, 1) time(s)—8 (10, 8) sts.

Cut yarn, leaving a 5-inch tail. Using tapestry needle, thread tail through rem sts and pull tight. Weave in all ends. Block as necessary.

Right Mitten

Work as for left mitten to thumb gusset.

Thumb gusset

Rnd 1: K22 (30, 37), pm, M1, knit to end of rnd—31 (41, 51) sts.

Rnd 2: Knit to marker, slip marker, k1, M1, pm, knit to end—32 (42, 52) sts with 2 gusset sts between markers.

Work gusset and remainder of mitten as for left mitten. ●

COLOR KEY
- ■ A
- ■ B
- □ C
- ■ D
- □ E

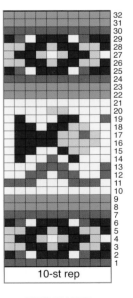

10-st rep

FISH CHART

Sweet Hearts

You won't find hearts sweeter than these! Inspired by colors girls love, she'll want to wear this not only on Valentine's Day, but every day.

Design by Simona Merchant-Desto

Skill Level
■■■□ INTERMEDIATE

Sizes
Child's extra-small (small, medium, large)
Instructions are given for smallest size, with larger sizes in parentheses. When only 1 number is given, it applies to all sizes.

Finished Measurements
Circumference: 14 (15½, 17½, 19¼) inches
Width: 4 inches + 2-inch earflap

Materials

- Plymouth Worsted Merino Superwash (worsted weight; 100% superwash fine merino wool; 218 yds/100g per skein): 1 skein each khaki #13 (A), lavender #18 (B), olive #12 (C), rose #30 (D) and violet #15 (E)
- Size 5 (3.75mm) 16-inch circular or double-point needles (set of 5) or size needed to obtain gauge
- Size 6 (4mm) 16-inch circular or double-point needles (set of 5) or size needed to obtain gauge
- Size D/3 (3.25mm) crochet hook
- 2 stitch holders
- Stitch marker

Gauge
23 sts and 28 rnds = 4 inches/10cm in 2-color stranded St st.

To save time, take time to check gauge.

Special Abbreviations
Place marker (pm): Place a marker on needle to separate sections.

Make 1 Left (M1L): Insert LH needle from front to back under the running thread between the last st worked and next st on LH needle; knit into the back of resulting loop.

Make 1 Right (M1R): Insert LH needle from back to front under the running thread between the last st worked and next st on LH needle. With RH needle, knit into the front of resulting loop.

Pattern Notes
Headband is worked from bottom of earflaps up.

Use double-point needles for smallest size and circular needle all other sizes.

Headband

Earflaps
Make 2

With A and larger needle, cast on 3 sts.

Beg Earflap Chart

Row 1 (WS): P3.

Row 2 (RS): K1, M1L, k1, M1R, k1—5 sts.

Complete chart, inc as indicated—17 sts.

Place sts on holder.

Band
With smaller needle(s) and A and using backward-loop method, cast on 10 (11, 14, 15) sts, knit across 1 set of earflap sts, cast on 27 (33, 39, 45) sts, knit across 2nd set of earflap sts, cast on 9 (10, 13, 14) sts, pm for beg of rnd and join, taking care not to twist sts—80 (88, 100, 108) sts.

Work 2 rnds in k2, p2 rib and on 2nd rnd, inc 0 (2, 0, 2) sts—80 (90, 100, 110) sts.

Change to larger needle(s).

Following chart, work Heart pat around.

Change to smaller needle(s) and A.

Work 1 rnd in St st and dec 0 (2, 0, 2) sts—80 (88, 100, 108) sts.

Work 2 rnds in k2, p2 rib.

Bind off loosely in rib.

Finishing
Weave in all ends.

Block to finished measurements.

Crochet Edging
With crochet hook and A, make a slip st in first st of beg of rnd of lower edge, ch 1, sc around headband and earflaps, working 3 sc for every 4 sts or rows, work slip st in first st to join. Cut yarn and fasten off. ●

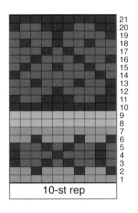

HEART CHART

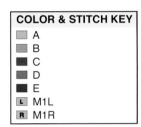

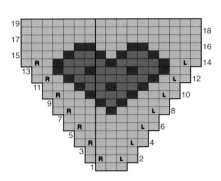

EARFLAP CHART

Oval Opulence

Echoing a bygone era of rich detail and texture, this hat is reminiscent of the illustrious 1920s cloche.

Design by Ann Weaver

Skill Level

⬛⬛⬛◻ INTERMEDIATE

Sizes

Adult's small/medium (medium/large)
Instructions are given for smaller size, with larger size in parentheses. When only 1 number is given, it applies to both sizes.

Finished Measurement

Circumference: 20 (22) inches

Materials

- Knitpicks Telemark (sport weight; 100% Peruvian highland wool; 103 yds/ 50g per ball): 1 ball each delft heather #24020 (A), brass heather #24023 (B), flame heather #24024 (C) and black #23926 (D)
- Size 6 (4mm) 16-inch circular needle or needle 3 sizes smaller than size needed to obtain gauge
- Size 9 (5.5mm) 16-inch circular and double-point needles (set of 4) or size needed to obtain gauge
- Stitch marker

Gauge

20 sts and 25 rnds = 4 inches/10cm in 2- or 3-color stranded St st with larger needle.

To save time, take time to check gauge.

Special Abbreviation

Knit in front and back (kfb): Knit in front and back of st to inc 1.

Pattern Stitch

Twisted Rib (even number of sts)
Rnd 1: *K1-tbl, p1; rep from * around.
Rep Rnd 1 for pat.

Pattern Note

When working in 3-color rounds, take care to carry yarn not in use loosely across back of work so that fabric doesn't pucker.

Hat

Using smaller circular needle and A, cast on 90 (100) sts; place marker for beg of rnd and join, being careful not to twist sts.

Work in Twisted Rib for 1½ inches.

Change to larger circular needle and St st.

Next rnd: [K9, kfb] 9 (10) times—100 (110) sts.

Following chart, work Beehive pat 10 (11) times around until 33-rnd chart is complete, shaping as indicated—20 (22) sts.

Cut B and draw through rem sts. Pull tight and fasten off.

Finishing

Weave in all ends. Wet-block to finished measurements. ●

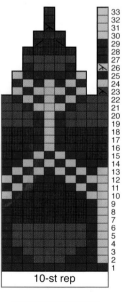

COLOR & STITCH KEY
⬛ K with A
◻ K with B
⬛ K with C
⬛ K with D
◪ Sk2p with C
◪ Sk2p with B
⬛ Ssk with D
⬛ K2tog with D
⬛ Sk2p with A

10-st rep

BEEHIVE CHART

Electric Butterfly

Redefine glamour when you wear these playful fingerless mitts made in vivid colors with a striking central butterfly.

Design by Jeannette Ehrich

Skill Level
■■■□ INTERMEDIATE

Sizes
Adult small/medium (medium/large) Instructions are given for smaller size, with larger size in parentheses. When only 1 number is given, it applies to both sizes.

Finished Measurements
Hand width: 4 (4½) inches
Hand length: 4¾ (5½) inches
Thumb length: ¾ (1) inch(es)

Materials
- Mirasol Tupa (DK weight; 50% merino wool/50% silk; 137 yds/50g per hank): 1 hank each azurite #812 (MC) and hot pink topaz #816 (CC)
- Size 2 (2.75mm) double-point needles (set of 4)
- Size 4 (3.5mm) double-point needles (set of 4) or size needed to obtain gauge

Gauge
29 sts and 30 rnds = 4 inches/10cm in 2-color stranded St st with larger needles.

To save time, take time to check gauge.

Special Abbreviations
N1, N2, N3: Needle 1, Needle 2 and Needle 3.

Make 1 Right (M1R): Take yarn in the fingers of your left hand, making a "thumbs up" sign with your hand. Bring your thumb over and then under yarn, creating a loop of yarn on your thumb. Turn your thumb slightly counterclockwise to bring your thumb closer to needle and place loop on needle.

Make 1 Left (M1L): Take yarn in the fingers of your right hand, making a "thumbs up" sign with your hand. Bring your thumb over and then under the yarn, creating a loop of yarn on your thumb. Turn your thumb slightly clockwise to bring your thumb closer to needle and place loop on needle.

Special Technique
2-Color Cast-On: Leaving 4-inch tails, make a slip knot on needle with both yarns held tog and MC to the right (these loops do not count as sts). Holding both yarns as you would for a long-tail cast-on, with MC over your thumb and CC over your index finger, cast on required number of sts. Slide slip knot off and gently pull ends to tighten first st.

Pattern Notes
Weave in the not-in-use yarn when carrying it more than 5 stitches. Catch the color you are carrying over and under the yarn you are knitting with. If weaving in yarns over multiple rounds, make sure to weave in the yarn on different stitches so that the stitches holding the woven-in yarns aren't stacked vertically. Maintain the same tension on both yarns—if you pull too tightly on the yarn that you are weaving in, your work will pucker or have significantly less stretch and flexibility in that area.

For a better-fitting mitten, measure the distance from the bottom of the wearer's palm to the crotch of her thumb. Work thumb gusset to that length.

Right Mitten

Cuff
Using 2-Color Cast-On method and smaller dpns, cast on 52 (56) sts. Distribute sts on 3 dpns as follows: 17-17-18 (19-19-18). Mark beg of rnd and join, taking care not to twist sts.

Work 20 rnds following Random Stripes Rib Chart.

Inc rnd: Change to larger dpns and MC; [k7, M1] 7 (0) times, k3 (k0), [k8, M1] 0 (7) times—59 (63) sts.

Redistribute sts on dpns as follows: 31-14-14 (33-15-15).

Thumb gusset

Rnd 1: Following charts for appropriate size, work as follows: N1: Work 31 (33) sts in Butterfly pat; N2 and N3: k1 MC, place marker, work 5 sts in Thumb Gusset pat, place marker, k1 MC, work 21 (23) sts following Palm Chart, beg and end where indicated on chart.

Rnd 2: Following charts, N1: Work Butterfly pat; N2 and N3: k1 MC, slip marker, work Thumb Gusset pat and inc as indicated, slip marker, k1 MC, working Palm pat to end of rnd—61 (65) sts.

Rnds 3–16 (18): Continue in established pats, working Butterfly pat on N1, 1 st MC outside markers and Thumb Gusset pat between markers (inc as indicated), and Palm pat to end—69 (73) sts with 15 sts between markers.

Note: If necessary for proper fit, work thumb gusset for more or fewer rnds (see Pattern Note).

Next rnd: N1: Work in pat; N2 and N3: k1 MC; sl 15 thumb gusset sts to waste yarn; using backward-loop method, cast on 5 sts in established Palm pat following chart, work in established Palm pat to end—59 (63) sts.

Continue in established Butterfly pat on N1 and Palm pat on N2 and N3 until 33- (37-) rnd Butterfly Chart is complete. Cut CC.

Dec rnd: Change to smaller dpns and MC; N1: k1, ssp, k2tog, p1, [k1, p1] 10 (11) times, ssk, p2tog, k1; N2 and N3: ssp, [k1, p1] 12 (13) times, k2tog—53 (57) sts.

Work 3 rnds in established k1, p1 rib.

Bind off in rib; cut yarn, leaving an 8-inch tail.

Thumb

Distribute gusset sts as follows on larger dpns: place first 6 gusset sts on N1; place next 8 sts on N2; place last st on N3, then working in established Palm pat, pick up and knit 2 sts in corner of gusset and 5 sts along cast-on edge; with spare needle and working in pat, pick up and knit 2 sts in gusset corner, work in pat across N1; work in pat across N2 and N3, mark beg of rnd—24 sts with 8 sts on each needle.

Dec rnd: N1: Ssk MC, work Palm pat to end; N2: work Palm pat; N3: ssk in pat, work Palm pat to last 2 sts, k2tog in pat—21 sts.

Work 4 (6) more rnds in pat. Cut CC.

Switch to smaller dpns and MC; work 2 rnds in k1, p1 rib and dec 1 st on first rnd—20 sts.

Bind off in pat. Cut yarn, leaving an 8-inch tail.

Weave in all ends. Block as desired.

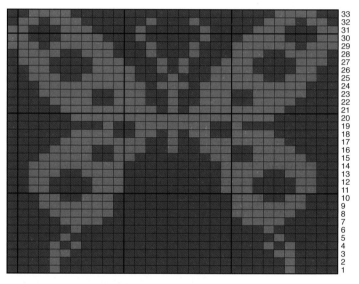

BUTTERFLY CHART (S/M)

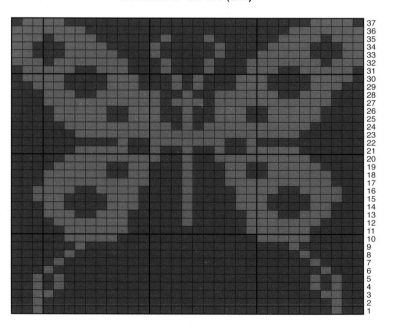

BUTTERFLY CHART (M/L)

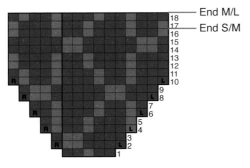

18 — End M/L
17 — End S/M
16
15
14
13
12
11
10
9
8
7
6
5
4
3
2
1

THUMB GUSSET CHART
(RIGHT MITTEN)

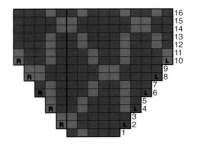

16
15
14
13
12
11
10
9
8
7
6
5
4
3
2
1

THUMB GUSSET CHART
(LEFT MITTEN S/M)

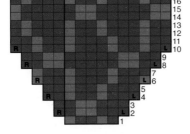

18
17
16
15
14
13
12
11
10
9
8
7
6
5
4
3
2
1

THUMB GUSSET CHART
(LEFT MITTEN M/L)

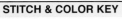

STITCH & COLOR KEY
■ MC
■ CC
■ P with MC
L M1L with indicated color
R M1R with indicated color

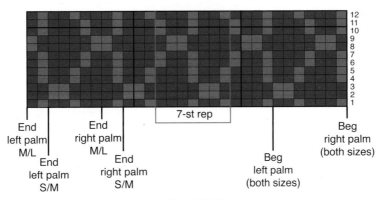

12
11
10
9
8
7
6
5
4
3
2
1

7-st rep

End left palm M/L
End left palm S/M
End right palm M/L
End right palm S/M
Beg left palm (both sizes)
Beg right palm (both sizes)

PALM CHART

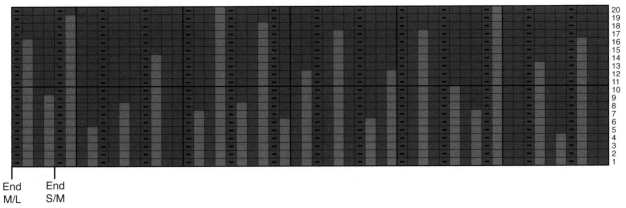

20
19
18
17
16
15
14
13
12
11
10
9
8
7
6
5
4
3
2
1

End M/L
End S/M

RANDOM STRIPES RIB CHART

Left Mitten

Work as for right mitten to beg of thumb gusset.

Thumb gusset

Rnd 1: Following charts for appropriate size, work as follows: N1: Work 31 (33) sts in Butterfly pat; N2 and N3: Work 21 (23) sts in Palm pat, beg and end where indicated on chart; k1 MC, place marker, work 5 sts in Thumb Gusset pat, place marker, k1 MC.

Rnd 2: Following charts, N1: Work Butterfly pat; N2 and N3: Work Palm pat to 1 st before marker, k1 MC, slip marker, work Thumb Gusset pat and inc as indicated, slip marker, k1 MC—61 (65) sts.

Rnds 3–16 (18): Continue in established pats, working Butterfly pat on N1; 21 (23) sts in Palm pat, 1 st MC outside markers and Thumb Gusset pat between markers (inc as indicated)—69 (73) sts with 15 sts between markers.

Note: If gusset length was revised for right mitten, make same changes for left mitten.

Next rnd: N1: Work in pat; N2 and N3: Work established Palm pat to marker, remove markers and sl 15 thumb gusset sts to waste yarn; using backward-loop method, cast on 5 sts in established Palm pat following chart, work last st in Palm pat—59 (63) sts.

Complete as for right mitten. •

Stitch & Color Techniques

Working From Charts

When working with more than one color in a row or round, sometimes a chart is provided to follow the pattern. On the chart, each square represents one stitch. A key is given indicating the color or stitch represended by each color or symbol in the box.

When working in rows, right-side rows are read from right to left, and wrong-side rows are read from left to right.

When working in rounds, every row on the chart is a right-side row and is read from right to left. The placement of the number on the chart indicates the beginning of the row or round.

Stranded or Fair Isle Knitting

Changing colors of yarn within the round or row is called stranded or Fair Isle knitting, and is most commonly worked in the round. This type of knitting can be worked either with both yarns in one hand, as shown in the photo to the right, or with one yarn in each hand. Carry the yarns along the wrong side of the fabric, working each color in the order indicated by the pattern. One color should always be carried under the other, whether you are knitting or purling—the strands will run parallel on the wrong side, as shown below. They should never change positions; if they do, it will be apparent on the right side of the fabric. If working back and forth, carry both yarns to the end of each row and twist to "lock" them in position on the last stitch. When working in

the round, there is no need to twist the yarns at the end of every round.

When one of the yarns is carried across the back for more than five stitches (or about an inch), the yarn should be caught into the back of one of the stitches that is worked with the other yarn. This will prevent snags caused by long floats.

Fair Isle knitting creates a denser fabric than plain stockinette-stitch knitting. Always work your gauge swatch in pattern before beginning your project. Watch your tension, ensuring that the stranded yarn is not pulled too tight; this will create puckers on the front of the fabric.

Knitting Basics

Long-Tail Cast-On

Leaving an end about an inch long for each stitch to be cast on, make a slip knot on the right needle.

Place the thumb and index finger of your left hand between the yarn ends with the long yarn end over your thumb, and the strand from the skein over your index finger. Close your other fingers over the strands to hold them against your palm. Spread your thumb and index fingers apart and draw the yarn into a "V."

Place the needle in front of the strand around your thumb and bring it underneath this strand. Carry the needle over and under the strand on your index finger.

Draw through loop on thumb.

Drop the loop from your thumb and draw up the strand to form a stitch on the needle.

Repeat until you have cast on the number of stitches indicated in the pattern. Remember to count the beginning slip knot as a stitch.

Cable Cast-On

This type of cast-on is used when adding stitches in the middle or at the end of a row.

Make a slip knot on the left needle. Knit a stitch in this knot and place it on the left needle. Insert the right needle between the last two stitches on the left needle. Knit a stitch and place it on the left needle. Repeat for each stitch needed.

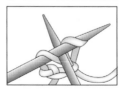

Increase (inc)

Two stitches in one stitch

Knit increase (kfb)

Knit the next stitch in the usual manner, but don't remove the stitch from the left needle. Place right needle behind left needle and knit again into the back of the same stitch. Slip original stitch off left needle.

Purl increase (pfb)

Purl the next stitch in the usual manner, but don't remove the stitch from the left needle. Place right needle behind left needle and purl again into the back of the same stitch. Slip original stitch off left needle.

Invisible Increase (M1)

There are several ways to make or increase one stitch.

Make 1 with Left Twist (M1L)

Insert left needle from front to back under the horizontal loop between the last stitch worked and next stitch on left needle.

With right needle, knit into the back of this loop.

To make this increase on the purl side, insert left needle in same manner and purl into the back of the loop.

Make 1 with Right Twist (M1R)

Insert left needle from back to front under the horizontal loop between the last stitch worked and next stitch on left needle.

With right needle, knit into the front of this loop.

To make this increase on the purl side, insert left needle in same manner and purl into the front of the loop.

Make **1** with Backward Loop over the right needle

With your thumb, make a loop over the right needle.

Slip the loop from your thumb onto the needle and pull to tighten.

Make **1** in top of stitch below

Insert tip of right needle into the stitch on left needle one row below.

Knit this stitch, then knit the stitch on the left needle.

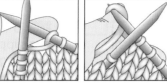

Decrease (dec)

Knit 2 together (k2tog)

Put tip of right needle through next two stitches on left needle as to knit. Knit these two stitches as one.

Purl 2 together (p2tog)

Put tip of right needle through next two stitches on left needle as to purl. Purl these two stitches as one.

Slip, Slip, Knit (ssk)

Slip next two stitches, one at a time, as to knit from left needle to right needle.

Insert left needle in front of both stitches and knit them together.

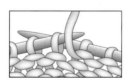

Slip, Slip, Purl (ssp)

Slip next two stitches, one at a time, as to knit from left needle to right needle. Slip these stitches back onto left needle keeping them twisted. Purl these two stitches together through back loops.

Kitchener Stitch

This method of weaving with two needles is used for the toes of socks and flat seams. To weave the edges together and form an unbroken line of stockinette stitch, divide all stitches evenly onto two knitting needles—one behind the other. Thread yarn into tapestry needle. Hold needles with wrong sides together and work from right to left as follows:

Step 1:

Insert tapestry needle into first stitch on front needle as to purl. Draw yarn through stitch, leaving stitch on knitting needle.

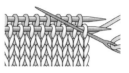

Step 1

Step 2:

Insert tapestry needle into the first stitch on the back needle as to purl. Draw yarn through stitch and slip stitch off knitting needle.

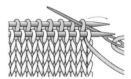

Step 2

Step 3:

Insert tapestry needle into the next stitch on same (back) needle as to knit, leaving stitch on knitting needle.

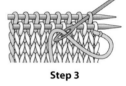

Step 3

Step 4:

Insert tapestry needle into the first stitch on the front needle as to knit. Draw yarn through stitch and slip stitch off knitting needle.

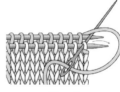

Step 4

Step 5:

Insert tapestry needle into the next stitch on same (front) needle as to purl. Draw yarn through stitch, leaving stitch on knitting needle.

Repeat Steps 2 through 5 until one stitch is left on each needle. Then repeat Steps 2 and 4. Fasten off. Woven stitches should be the same size as adjacent knitted stitches.

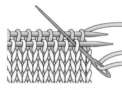

Step 5

- 17 accessory projects ranging from the simplest two-color methods, up to more advanced techniques employing three or more colors.

- Projects presented from simplest to advanced, along with easy-to-follow, step-by-step photographic tutorials.

- Great starting point for knitters ready to dive into their first stranded colorwork project.

U.S. $14.95 CANADA $17.95

UPC

0 54525 22090 0

PRINTED IN USA
AnniesAttic.com

EAN
ISBN: 978-1-59217-337-2

51495

9 781592 173372

JIAN ®

Academic Version

Erika Matulich

MarketingBuilder

Express

From the JIAN family of best-selling and award-winning software

This workbook provides the tools to write a profitable sales and marketing plan

- *Market Analysis*
- *Marketing Communications*
- *Sales Plan*

MarketingBuilder *Express*
SOFTWARE INCLUDED